I0006501

NIST Special Publication 800-107
Revision 1

Recommendation for Applications Using Approved Hash Algorithms

Quynh Dang

Computer Security Division
Information Technology Laboratory

COMPUTER SECURITY

August 2012

U.S. Department of Commerce
Rebecca M. Blank, Acting Secretary

National Institute of Standards and Technology

Patrick Gallagher, Under Secretary of Commerce for Standards and Technology and Director

Abstract

Hash functions that compute a fixed-length message digest from arbitrary length messages are widely used for many purposes in information security. This document provides security guidelines for achieving the required or desired security strengths when using cryptographic applications that employ the approved hash functions specified in Federal Information Processing Standard (FIPS) 180-4. These include functions such as digital signatures, Keyed-hash Message Authentication Codes (HMACs) and Hash-based Key Derivation Functions (Hash-based KDFs).

KEY WORDS: digital signatures, hash algorithm, hash function, hash-based key derivation algorithms, hash value, HMAC, message digest, randomized hashing, random number generation, SHA, truncated hash values.

Acknowledgements

The author, Quynh Dang of the National Institute of Standards and Technology (NIST) gratefully appreciates the contributions and comments from Elaine Barker, William E. Burr, Shu-jen Chang, Lily Chen, Donna F. Dodson, Morris Dworkin, John Kelsey, Ray Perlner, W. Timothy Polk and Andrew Regenscheid. The author also appreciates comments from Daniel Brown, Hugo Krawczyk, Praveen Gauravaram and Richard Davis during the development of this Recommendation.

Table of Contents

Recommendation for Applications Using Approved Hash Algorithms

1 Introduction

A hash algorithm is used to map a message of arbitrary length to a fixed-length message digest. Federal Information Processing Standard (FIPS) 180-4, the Secure Hash Standard (SHS) [FIPS 180-4], specifies seven approved hash algorithms: SHA-1, SHA-224, SHA-256, SHA-384, SHA-512, SHA-512/224 and SHA-512/256.

This Recommendation provides security guidelines for supporting the required or desired security strengths of several cryptographic applications that employ the approved hash functions specified in FIPS 180-4, such as digital signature applications specified in FIPS 186-3 [FIPS 186-3], Keyed-hash Message Authentication Codes (HMACs) specified in FIPS 198-1 [FIPS 198-1] and Hash-based Key Derivation Functions specified in SP 800-56A [SP 800-56A] and SP 800-56B [SP 800-56B]. While the use of hash functions in HMAC-based key derivation functions is specified in SP 800-56C [SP 800-56C] and SP 800-108 [SP 800-108], these documents sufficiently address the security aspects of their use, so discussions of SP 800-56C and SP 800-108 are not included herein.

2 Authority

This Recommendation has been developed by the National Institute of Standards and Technology (NIST) in furtherance of its statutory responsibilities under the Federal Information Security Management Act (FISMA) of 2002, Public Law 107-347.

NIST is responsible for developing standards and guidelines, including minimum requirements, for providing adequate information security for all agency operations and assets, but such standards and guidelines shall not apply to national security systems. This recommendation is consistent with the requirements of the Office of Management and Budget (OMB) Circular A-130, Section 8b(3), Securing Agency Information Systems, as analyzed in A-130, Appendix IV: Analysis of Key Sections. Supplemental information is provided in A-130, Appendix III.

This Recommendation has been prepared for use by Federal agencies. It may be used by non-governmental organizations on a voluntary basis and is not subject to copyright (attribution would be appreciated by NIST).

Nothing in this Recommendation should be taken to contradict standards and guidelines made mandatory and binding on Federal agencies by the Secretary of Commerce under statutory authority. Nor should this Recommendation be interpreted as altering or superseding the existing authorities of the Secretary of Commerce, Director of the OMB, or any other federal official.

Conformance testing for implementations of this Recommendation will be conducted within the framework of the Cryptographic Algorithm Validation Program (CAVP) and the Cryptographic Module Validation Program (CMVP). The requirements of this Recommendation are indicated by the word "**shall**". Some of these requirements may be out-of-scope for CAVP and CMVP validation testing, and thus are the responsibility of entities using, implementing, installing, or configuring applications that incorporate this Recommendation.

3 Glossary of Terms, Acronyms and Mathematical Symbols

3.1 Terms and Definitions

Adversary	An entity that is not authorized to access or modify information, or who works to defeat any protections afforded the information.
Algorithm	A clearly specified mathematical process for computation; a set of rules that, if followed, will give a prescribed result.
Approved	FIPS-approved and/or NIST-recommended. An algorithm or technique that is either 1) specified in a FIPS or NIST Recommendation, 2) adopted in a FIPS or NIST Recommendation or 3) specified in a list of NIST-approved security functions.
Approved hash algorithms	Hash algorithms specified in FIPS 180-4.
Bit string	An ordered sequence of 0 and 1 bits. In this Recommendation, the leftmost bit is the most significant bit of the string. The rightmost bit is the least significant bit of the string.
Bits of security	See security strength.
Block cipher	An invertible symmetric-key cryptographic algorithm that operates on fixed-length blocks of input using a secret key and an unvarying transformation algorithm. The resulting output block is the same length as the input block.
Collision	An event in which two different messages have the same message digest.
Collision resistance	An expected property of a hash function whereby it is computationally infeasible to find a collision, See "Collision".

Digital signature	The result of applying two cryptographic functions (a hash function, followed by a digital signature function; see FIPS 186-3 for details). When the functions are properly implemented, the digital signature provides origin authentication, data integrity protection and signatory non-repudiation.
Hash algorithm	See hash function. "Hash algorithm" and "hash function" are used interchangeably in this Recommendation.
Hash function	A function that maps a bit string of arbitrary length to a fixed-length bit string. The function is expected to have the following three properties:

      1. Collision resistance (see Collision resistance),

      2. Preimage resistance (see Preimage resistance) and

      3. Second preimage resistance (see Second preimage resistance).

Approved hash functions are specified in [FIPS 180-4].

Hash output	See "message digest".
Hash value	See "message digest".
Key	A parameter used with a cryptographic algorithm that determines its operation in such a way that an entity with knowledge of the key can reproduce or reverse the operation, while an entity without knowledge of the key cannot. Examples applicable to this Recommendation include:

      1. The computation of a keyed-hash message authentication code.

      2. The verification of a keyed-hash message authentication code.

      3. The generation of a digital signature on a message.

      4. The verification of a digital signature.

Key Derivation Key	A key used as an input to a key derivation function to derive other keys.
Keying Material	A bit string, such that any non-overlapping segments of the string with the required lengths can be used as symmetric cryptographic keys and secret parameters, such as initialization vectors.
L-bit Hash Function	A hash function for which the length of the output is L bits.
MAC algorithm	An algorithm that computes a MAC from a message and a key.

Message digest	The result of applying a hash function to a message. Also known as a "hash value" or "hash output".
Preimage	A message X that produces a given message digest when it is processed by a hash function.
Preimage resistance	An expected property of a hash function such that, given a randomly chosen message digest, *message_digest*, it is computationally infeasible to find a preimage of the *message_digest*, See "Preimage".
Random bit	A bit for which an attacker has exactly a 50% probability of success of guessing the value of the bit as either a zero or one. It is also called an unbiased bit.
Random bit generator	A device or algorithm that can produce a sequence of bits that appear to be both statistically independent and unbiased.
Randomized hashing	A process by which the input to a hash function is randomized before being processed by the hash function.
Random number	A value in a set of numbers that has an equal probability of being selected from the total population of possibilities and, in that sense, is unpredictable. A random number is an instance of an unbiased random variable, that is, the output produced by a uniformly distributed random process. Random numbers may, e.g., be obtained by converting suitable stings of random bits (see [SP 800-90A], Appendix B.5 for details).
Second preimage	A message X', that is different from a given message X, such that its message digest is the same as the known message digest of X.
Second preimage resistance	An expected property of a hash function whereby it is computationally infeasible to find a second preimage of a known message digest, See "Second preimage".
Secret keying material	The binary data that is used to form secret keys, such as AES encryption or HMAC keys.
Security strength (Also "bits of security")	A number associated with the amount of work (that is, the number of operations) that is required to break a cryptographic algorithm or system. If 2^N execution operations of the algorithm (or system) are required to break the cryptographic algorithm, then the security strength is N bits.
Shall	Used to indicate a requirement of this Recommendation.
Shared secret	A secret value that has been computed using a key agreement algorithm and is used as input to a key derivation function.

3.2 Acronyms

FIPS   Federal Information Processing Standard

SHA   Secure Hash Algorithm

KDF   Key Derivation Function

MAC   Message Authentication Code

HMAC   Keyed-hash Message Authentication Code

RBG   Random Bit Generator

3.3 Symbols

K HMAC key.

L Length in bits of the full message digest from a hash function.

MacTag   Transmitted full or truncated HMAC output.

$\min(x, y)$ The minimum of x and y. For example, if $x < y$, then $\min(x, y) = x$.

λ The length in bits of a *MacTag*, or the length in bits of a truncated message digest (used, for example, by a digital signature algorithm).

4 Approved Hash Algorithms

Currently, there are seven approved hash algorithms specified in FIPS 180-4: SHA-1, SHA-224, SHA-256, SHA-384 SHA-512, SHA-512/224 and SHA-512/256. These hash algorithms produce outputs of 160, 224, 256, 384, 512, 224 and 256 bits, respectively. The output of a hash algorithm is commonly known as a message digest, a hash value or a hash output.

4.1 Hash Function Properties

An approved hash function[1] is expected to have the following three properties:

1. Collision resistance: It is computationally infeasible to find two different inputs to the hash function that have the same hash value. That is, if *hash* is a hash function, it is computationally infeasible to find two different inputs x and x' for which $hash(x) = hash(x')$. Collision resistance is measured by the amount of work that would be needed to find a collision for a hash function with high probability. If the amount of work is 2^N, then the collision resistance is N bits. The expected collision-resistance strength of a hash function is half the length of the hash value produced by that hash function, i.e., for an L-bit hash function, the expected security strength for collision resistance is $L/2$ bits. For example, SHA-256 produces a (full-length) hash value of 256 bits; SHA-256 provides an expected collision resistance of 128 bits (see Table 1 in Section 4.2).

---

[1] The terms "hash function" and "hash algorithm" are used interchangeably, depending on the context of the discussions throughout this Recommendation.

2. Preimage resistance[2]: Given a randomly chosen hash value, *hash_value*, it is computationally infeasible to find an *x* so that *hash(x)* = *hash_value*. This property is also called the one-way property. Preimage resistance is measured by the amount of work that would be needed to have a high probability of finding a preimage for a hash function. If the amount of work is 2^N, then the preimage resistance is *N* bits. The expected preimage-resistance strength of a hash function is the length of the hash value produced by that hash function, i.e., for an *L*-bit hash function, the expected security strength for preimage resistance is *L* bits. For example, SHA-256 produces a (full-length) hash value of 256 bits; SHA-256 provides an expected preimage resistance of 256 bits (see Table 1 in Section 4.2).

3. Second preimage resistance: It is computationally infeasible to find a second input that has the same hash value as any other specified input. That is, given an input *x*, it is computationally infeasible to find a second input *x'* that is different from *x*, such that *hash(x)* = *hash(x')*. Second preimage resistance is measured by the amount of work that would be needed to have a high probability of finding a second preimage for a hash function. If the amount of work is 2^N, then the second preimage resistance is *N* bits. In general, the expected second preimage strength of a hash function is the length of the hash value produced by that hash function, i.e., for an *L*-bit hash function, the expected security strength for second preimage resistance is *L* bits. For example, SHA-256 produces a (full-length) hash value of 256 bits; SHA-256 provides an expected second preimage resistance of 256 bits (see Table 1 in Section 4.2). However, for some hash functions, the second preimage resistance strength also depends on the message length processed by the hash function. More details can be found in Appendix A.

The security strength of a hash function is determined by its collision resistance strength, preimage resistance strength or second preimage resistance strength, depending on the property(ies) that the cryptographic application needs from the hash function. If an application requires more than one property from the hash function, then the weakest property is the security strength of the hash function for that application. For instance, the security strength of a hash function for digital signatures is defined as its collision resistance strength, because digital signatures require both collision resistance and second preimage resistance from the hash function, and the collision resistance strength of the hash function (*L*/2) is less than its second preimage resistance strength (i.e., *L*).

A hash function that is not suitable for one application might be suitable for other cryptographic applications that do not require the same security properties. SHA-1 is not suitable for general-purpose digital signature applications (as specified in FIPS 186-3) that require 112 bits of security. In the case of digital signatures, SHA-1 does not provide the 112 bits of collision resistance (see Table 1 in Section 4.2) needed to achieve the security strength. On the other hand, SHA-1 does provide the 112 bits of preimage resistance that is needed to achieve the 112-bit security strength for HMAC. The security strengths of the approved hash functions for different applications can be found in SP 800-57, Part 1 [SP 800-57].

---

[2] There are slightly different definitions of preimage resistance of hash functions in the literature.

4.2 Strengths of the Approved Hash Algorithms

Table 1 provides a summary of the security strengths for the hash function security properties (discussed in the previous section) of the approved hash functions.

Table 1: **Strengths of the Security Properties of the Approved Hash Algorithms**

	SHA-1	SHA-224	SHA-256	SHA-384	SHA-512	SHA-512/224	SHA-512/256
Collision Resistance Strength in bits	< 80	112	128	192	256	112	128
Preimage Resistance Strength in bits	160	224	256	384	512	224	256
Second Preimage Resistance Strength in bits	105-160	201-224	201-256	384	394-512	224	256

As mentioned in Section 4.1, the expected collision resistance strength of any approved hash function is, in general, half the length of its hash value. This is currently believed to be true for all the approved hash functions except SHA-1. The latest cryptanalytic results for SHA-1 [SHA1 Attack] indicate that it may have a collision resistance strength that is considerably less than its expected strength of 80 bits.

The expected preimage resistance strengths of the approved hash functions are provided in the above table. At the time that this Recommendation was written, there had been no known short cuts for finding preimages of the hash values generated by the approved hash algorithms.

Except for SHA-384, SHA-512/224 and SHA-512/256, the second preimage resistance strengths of the approved hash functions depend not only on the functions themselves, but also on the sizes of the messages that the hash functions process [Second Preimage Attack]. In Table 1, the low end of each range applies to the situation where the length of the message input to the hash function is the maximum length allowed by the hash function, while the high end of the range applies to the situation where the message input length is relatively small. Information on determining the actual second preimage resistance strengths of the approved hash functions for different message lengths is provided in Appendix A. In the case of SHA-384, SHA-512/224 or SHA-512/256, the second preimage resistance strength does not depend on the message length; details can be found in Appendix A.

Note that the preimage resistance and the second preimage resistance strengths are greater than the collision resistance strength for each of the approved hash algorithms specified in FIPS 180-4.

5 Hash function Usage

5.1 Truncated Message Digest

Some applications may require a value that is shorter than the (full-length) message digest provided by an approved hash function as specified in FIPS 180-4. In such cases, it may be appropriate to use a subset of the bits produced by the hash function as the (shortened) message digest.

Let the (shortened) message digest be called a truncated message digest, and let λ be its desired length in bits. A truncated message digest may be used if the following requirements are met:

1. The length of the output block of the approved hash function to be used **shall** be greater than λ (i.e., $L > \lambda$).

2. The λ left-most bits of the full-length message digest **shall** be selected as the truncated message digest.

   For example, if a truncated message digest of 96 bits is desired, the SHA-256 hash function could be used (e.g., because it is available to the application, and provides an output larger than 96 bits). The leftmost 96 bits of the 256-bit message digest generated by SHA-256 are selected as the truncated message digest, and the rightmost 160 bits of the message digest are discarded.

3. If collision resistance is required, λ **shall** be at least twice the required collision resistance strength s (in bits) for the truncated message digest (i.e., $\lambda \geq 2s$).

These specifications for truncating the output of a cryptographic hash function promote application interoperability in situations where the use of shortened message digests is appropriate (and permissible), as determined by implementers and application developers acting in conformance with NIST Standards and Recommendations.

Truncating the message digest can impact the security of an application. By truncating a message digest, the expected collision resistance strength is reduced from $L/2$ to $\lambda/2$ (in bits). For the example in item 2 above, even though SHA-256 provides 128 bits of collision resistance, the collision resistance provided by the 96-bit truncated message digest is half the length of the truncated message digest, which is 48 bits, in this case.

The truncated message digest of λ bits provides an expected preimage resistance of λ bits, not L bits, regardless of the hash function used.

The expected second preimage resistance strength of a message digest truncated to λ bits sometimes depends on the length of the message. This dependence is determined as specified in Appendix A. Note that there are situations for which the expected second preimage resistance strength does not depend on the message length. For example, a 130-bit truncated message digest generated using SHA-256 has an expected second preimage strength of 130 bits, rather than a value in the range specified in Table 1 above for SHA-256.

Truncating the message digest can have other impacts, as well. For example, applications that use a truncated message digest risk attacks based on confusion between different parties about the specific amount of truncation used, as well as the specific hash function that was used to produce the truncated message digest. Any application using a truncated message digest is responsible for ensuring that the truncation amount and the hash function used are known to all parties, with no chance of ambiguity.

5.2   Digital Signatures

A hash function is used to map a message of any eligible length (see FIPS 180-4) to a fixed-length message digest. In a digital signature generation process, this message digest is then signed by a signing operation, such as an RSA private key operation, to produce a digital signature. The resulting digital signature is used to verify who signed the message and whether or not the message was altered (either deliberately or accidentally) after it was signed.

When two different messages have the same message digest (i.e., a collision is found), then a digital signature of one message could be used as a digital signature for the other message. If this happens, then a verified digital signature does not guarantee the authenticity of the signed message, because either one of the two messages could be considered valid. Therefore, a hash function used for digital signatures requires collision resistance. The approved hash functions are considered to provide the collision resistance strengths as specified in Table 1 of Section 4.2.

For digital signature applications, the security strength of a hash function without any preprocessing is generally its collision resistance strength. When appropriate processing is applied to the data before the hash value is computed, the security strength may be more than the collision resistance strength (see Section 5.2.3).

Without any preprocessing of the message input to the hash function, the security strength of any digital signature that is generated using an algorithm specified in FIPS 186-3 is the minimum of the collision resistance strength of the hash algorithm and the security strength provided by the signing algorithm. More information on security strengths can be found in SP 800-57, Part 1. For instance, if a digital signature that is generated by one of the approved digital signature algorithms with SHA-1 as the hash function and key sizes specified in FIPS 186-3[3], then the security strength of this digital signature is less than 80 bits (see Table 1 in Section 4.2); i.e., the strength of the digital signature process is determined by the strength of SHA-1, rather than the strength of the key, in this case. Therefore, SHA-1 **shall not** be used in any new digital signature applications that require at least 80 bits of security strength. Furthermore, SHA-1 **shall not** be used for the generation of digital signatures after the end of 2013 (see SP 800-131A [SP 800-131A] for information about the required key lengths for digital signature applications). More information on the security strengths of digital signature applications using the approved hash algorithms and the recommended lifetimes of cryptographic algorithm usage can be found in SP 800-57, Part 1.

There are several ways to use hash functions with digital signature algorithms as described below.

5.2.1 Full-length Message Digests

When the untruncated output of an approved hash function (as specified in FIPS 180-4) is used by an approved digital signature algorithm (as specified in FIPS 186-3), the resulting full-length message digests can support security strengths up to those given in Table 1 of Section 4.2 (for collision resistance).

5.2.2 Truncated Message Digests

In some specific situations, truncated message digests are used in generating digital signatures. (Details about these situations, including the lengths required for the truncated hash values, can be found in FIPS 186-3.) In such cases, the security strength that can be supported by a hash function depends on the length of these truncated values, as well as the particular hash function that is used.

As noted in Section 5.1, when the outputs of an approved L-bit hash function are truncated to λ bits (where $\lambda < L$), the collision resistance strength supported by the truncated message digests is reduced to $\lambda /2$ bits. Therefore, in addition to the requirements/restrictions imposed by FIPS 186-3, the value of λ **shall** be at least twice the desired security strength (in bits) required for the digital signature.

For example, if a security strength of 112 bits is required for digital signatures, a (truncated) message digest of (at least) 224 bits must be used. If required/desired, any approved hash functions except SHA-1 could be employed to generate (truncated) message digests of exactly 224 bits in length. (For SHA-224 and SHA-512/224, the hash function's output would not require truncation.) It is recommended that the hash function chosen should minimize the number of truncation operations required to achieve the required/desired length for the hash value. For the 224-bit example above, SHA-512/224 should be chosen over SHA-384 and SHA-512/256. All three hash functions employ one (internal) truncation operation to produce their output, but SHA-384 and SHA-512/256 would each require an additional (external) truncation operation to pare their output down to the desired length of 224 bits.

---

[3] Key sizes that provide at least 112 bits of strength are provided.

5.2.3 Randomized Hashing for Digital Signatures

As described in Section 5.2, the overall security strength of a digital signature is limited by the collision resistance strength of the hash function. However, when using the randomized hashing technique specified in SP 800-106 [SP 800-106], a randomized hash function may support a higher level of security with respect to a particular potential vulnerability, offering enhanced protection to a message signer against a collision attack by a malicious message preparer who formulates the message to be signed, but does not actually sign the message.

In such an attack, the malicious message preparer would endeavor to find two messages that hash to the same value. Once the message signer had generated a signature for one of the messages, the malicious preparer could accuse the signer of having signed the other message instead.

In situations where one party is asked to sign messages prepared by another party, the level of protection (in bits) that is provided to the message signer against a collision attack by using randomized hashing is determined by the minimum of the following three quantities:

- The second preimage resistance strength (in bits) of the hash function.

- The security strength (in bits) of the random bit generator (RBG) employed by the signer to produce bit strings used to randomize messages, or, the collision resistance strength (in bits) of the hash function – whichever is larger.

- The sum of the collision resistance strength (in bits) of the hash function and the smaller of these two quantities:
    - (1) The length (in bits) of bit strings used to randomize messages (denoted rv in SP 800-106), and
    - (2) The length (in bits) of the RBG output used to generate rv (as specified in Section 3.3 of SP 800-106).

When randomized hashing is used, the RBG (see Section 5.5 below for more information) employed to produce the bit strings used to randomize messages **shall** support a security strength that is equal to or greater than the security strength of the signing algorithm. See SP 800-57, Part 1, for information about security strengths of different signing algorithms. The randomization process itself **shall** conform to the specifications of SP 800-106 for digital signature applications supporting at least 112 bits of security. Under these conditions, SHA-1-based randomized hashing could provide 112 bits of security strength against a collision attack by a malicious message preparer, even though the unrandomized SHA-1 function has a collision resistance strength that is less than 80 bits.

It is important to note what the use of randomized hashing for digital signatures does and does not provide:

  1)   Randomized hashing can offer a message signer additional protection by reducing the likelihood that a message preparer can find multiple messages that yield the same hash value during the digital signature

generation process – even if it is practical to find collisions for the unrandomized hash function.

2)   Randomized hashing does not offer the message preparer or the signature verifiers any additional protection from a misbehaving signer (who may, for example, generate one signature that can be associated with either of two chosen messages after finding randomized versions of those messages that hash to the same value).

3)   Randomized hashing does not improve the assurance of origin authenticity, data integrity, and/or signatory non-repudiation provided by the digital signature to signature verifiers (i.e., relying parties).

5.3   Keyed-Hash Message Authentication Codes (HMAC)

5.3.1   Description

Message authentication codes (MACs) provide data authentication and integrity protection. Two types of algorithms for computing a MAC have been approved: 1) MAC algorithms that are based on approved block cipher algorithms (more information can be found in [SPs 800-38B, C and D]) and 2) MAC algorithms that are based on hash functions, called HMAC algorithms, that are specified in FIPS 198-1. This section discusses the use of HMAC.

An output from an HMAC algorithm is called an HMAC output. The HMAC output is either used in its entirety, or is truncated (see Section 5.3.3) when it is transmitted for subsequent verification. The transmitted value is called a *MacTag*. The HMAC algorithm requires the use of a secret key that is shared between the entity that generates the HMAC output (e.g., a message sender), and the entity (or entities) that need to verify the transmitted *MacTag* (message receiver(s)).

The HMAC output is generated from a secret key and the string of "text" to be MACed (e.g., a message to be sent) using the HMAC algorithm. The *MacTag* is provided to the *MacTag* verifier, along with the "text" that was MACed (e.g., the sender transmits both the *MacTag* and the message to the intended receiver).

The verifier computes an HMAC output on the received "text" using the same key and HMAC algorithm that were (purportedly) used to generate the received *MacTag*, generates a (new) *MacTag* (either a full or truncated HMAC output), and then compares the verifier-generated *MacTag* with the received *MacTag*. If the two values match, the "text" has been correctly received and the verifier is assured that the entity that generated the *MacTag* is a member of the community of users that share the key.

The security strength provided by the HMAC algorithm depends on the security strength of the HMAC key, the underlying hash algorithm and the length of the *MacTag*.

5.3.2   The HMAC Key

The security strength of the HMAC algorithm depends, in part, on the security strength of the HMAC key, K. An HMAC key **shall** have a security strength that meets or exceeds the security strength required to protect the data over which the HMAC is computed.

The HMAC key **shall** be kept secret. When the secrecy of the HMAC key, K, is not preserved, an adversary that knows K, may impersonate any of the users that share that key in order to generate *MacTags* that seem to be authentic (i.e., *MacTags* that can be verified and are subsequently presumed to be authentic).

HMAC keys **shall** be generated as specified in SP 800-133 [SP 800-133].

5.3.3 Truncation of HMAC Output

When an application truncates the HMAC output to generate a *MacTag* to a desired length, λ, the λ left-most bits of the HMAC output **shall** be used as the *MacTag*. However, the output length, λ, **shall** be no less than 32 bits. For example, a low bandwidth channel or a desired high efficiency computation application such as audio or video casting application might use 32-bit *MacTags*.

5.3.4 Security Effect of the HMAC Key

Let C denote the bit length of the internal hash value that is denoted H in FIPS 180-4. (This H is often called the "chaining value" in descriptions of Merkle–Damgård-style hash functions.) Note that C is not (necessarily) equal to L, the bit length of the hash function's output (see, for example, SHA-384 or SHA-512/t for any $t < 512$, for which $L < 512 = C$). In all currently approved hash functions, $L \leq C$ (with $L = C$ for SHA-1, SHA-256, and SHA-512).

The effective security strength[4] of the HMAC key is the minimum of the security strength of K and the value of $2C$. That is, *security strength* = min(*security strength of K*, $2C$). For example, if the security strength of K is 128 bits, and SHA-1 is used, then the effective security strength of the HMAC key is 128 bits, since for SHA-1, $2C = 320$. Note that, in this example, even if the security strength of K is greater than 320 bits, the effective security strength of the key is limited to 320 bits (the value of $2C$ for SHA-1). In general, there is no benefit in generating K with more than $2C$ bits of security. In particular, it is not sensible to generate K with a bit length that exceeds the input block size of the approved L-bit hash function employed in the HMAC construction. Such a K is hashed, and the resulting L-bit value is used instead. Returning to the SHA-1 example, suppose that the key K has a bit length greater than 512 (the input block size for SHA-1). Instead of using K directly, HMAC replaces K by its 160-bit SHA-1 hash value, and so the effective security strength of that choice of K is no more than 160 bits.

---

[4] As described in [BCK1], the success of a collision attack on any approved HMAC algorithm in FIPS 198-1 that uses SHA-1 would require the collection of at least 2^{80} pairs of chosen plaintexts and their corresponding HMAC values. This is an impractical task. So, the collision attack is not considered in this document. In this Recommendation, the strength of the HMAC key is considered to be the amount of work required for an attacker who performs a brute-force attack to discover the HMAC key K or the first hash values (Hs) from hashing the two strings:($K0 \oplus opad$) and ($K0 \oplus ipad$) separately in the HMAC construction (see FIPS 198-1) in order to generate authentic *MacTags* at any time.

5.3.5 Security of the HMAC Values

The successful verification of a *MacTag* does not completely guarantee that the accompanying text is authentic; there is a slight chance that an adversary with no knowledge of the HMAC key, K, can present a (*MacTag, text*) pair that will pass the verification procedure. From the perspective of an adversary that does not know the HMAC key K (i.e., the adversary is not among the community of users that share the key), the assurance of authenticity provided by a *MacTag* depends on its length and on the number of failed *MacTag* verifications allowed by a system for each value of the HMAC key.

Let 2^t be the number of failed *MacTag* verifications allowed by a system for each value of the HMAC key. The *MacTag* length, λ, and the value of t need to be chosen to avoid an unacceptable probability of falsely accepting forged data. The likelihood of accepting forged data as authentic is $(1/2)^{(\lambda - t)}$. For example, if λ is 32, and a system allows 2^{12} failed *MacTag* verifications for any given value of the HMAC key, then the likelihood of accepting forged data is $(1/2)^{20}$. In order to increase assurance of authenticity, either λ would need to be increased, or the number of allowed failed *MacTag* verifications for each value of the HMAC key would need to be decreased. To avoid having an unacceptable probability of falsely accepting forged data at any time, the value of the HMAC key must be changed to a new value before the number of failed *MacTag* authentications reaches the maximum allowed number (2^t). For the example above, with $\lambda = 32$ and $t = 20$, the HMAC key must be changed before the number of failed *MacTag* verifications reaches 2^{12}.

The table below provides the likelihoods of accepting forged data for different *MacTag* lengths and allowed numbers of MAC verifications using a given value of the HMAC key. This table is intended to assist the implementers of HMAC applications in security-sensitive systems to assess the security risk associated with using *MacTags*.

| λ | Number of Failed Verifications Allowed (2^t): | | |
	2^{20}	2^{30}	2^{35}
40	2^{-20}	2^{-10}	2^{-5}
64	2^{-44}	2^{-34}	2^{-29}
96	2^{-76}	2^{-66}	2^{-61}

Table 2: Risks/Likelihoods of Accepting Forged Data

Each 2^{-x} entry displayed in Table 2 is the probability of accepting forged data given the indicated choices for the *MacTag* length and the number of failed *MacTag* verifications allowed for a fixed value of the HMAC key. If the probability is not acceptable for the system, the HMAC key **shall** be changed to a new value before the number of failed MAC verifications reaches 2^t.

A commonly acceptable length for the *MacTag* is 64 bits; *MacTags* with lengths shorter than 64 bits are discouraged.

5.4　Hash-based Key Derivation Functions

Hash functions can be used as building blocks in key derivation functions (KDFs) (e.g., as specified in SP 800-56A, SP 800-56B, SP 800-56C and SP 800-108).

The KDFs specified in future versions of SPs 800-56A and B are expected to use the hash functions either directly or indirectly in an HMAC construction. The method specified in SP 800-56C is an additional approved method for key derivation purposes in SPs 800-56A and B. The key derivation functions in SP 800-56A, B and C are used to generate (i.e., derive) secret keying material from a shared secret computed during a key agreement transaction between communicating parties.

The hash-based KDFs specified in SP 800-108 use an HMAC construction and can be used either: (1) to derive keying material from an existing key, or (2) as a key-expansion step in the key derivation method specified in SP 800-56C.

In addition to the KDFs in SPs 800-56A, B and C, and in SP 800-108, there are several other allowed application-specific KDFs described in SP 800-135 [SP 800-135]. These application-specific KDFs are approved for use in their own protocols with specific conditions; see SP 800-135 for detailed information.

5.4.1　Using a Hash Function Directly for Key Derivation

This section discusses and provides security requirements for the KDFs in SP 800-56A and B that use the hash function directly as their building block (i.e., in the concatenation and ASN.1 KDFs). The KDFs derive the keying material from a shared secret computed during the key agreement transaction and other input attributes.

The security strength that can be provided by a derived key depends on the security strength of the asymmetric keys used to generate the shared secret, the preimage strength of the hash function used in the KDF and the length of the derived key. Therefore, if a derived key is intended to provide s bits of security strength, then each of the following **shall** be equal to or greater than s:

- The security strength supported by the asymmetric keys,
- The preimage strength of the hash function, and
- The length of the derived key in bits.

5.4.2　Using HMAC for Key Derivation During a Key Agreement Transaction

This section discusses and provides security requirements for the key derivation methods in SP 800-56A, B and C that use the hash function in an HMAC construction.

The KDFs specified in SPs 800-56A and B derive keys in a single step, and are being revised to allow the use of HMAC with an approved hash function for key derivation. SP 800-56C specifies a two-step key derivation procedure in which HMAC can be used during the key derivation process.

5.4.2.1　Using HMAC in the Single-Step Key Derivation Process

SP 800-56A and B specify single-step key derivation functions using HMAC in the concatenation and ASN.1 forms.

The security strength that can be provided by a derived key depends on the security strength of the asymmetric keys used to generate the shared secret, the preimage strength of the hash function used in the HMAC construction in the KDF and the length of the derived key. Note that in this case, the key used for HMAC is a salt, which can be a publicly known value, a secret value, or a combination of both. Therefore, if a derived key is intended to provide s bits of security strength, then each of the following **shall** be equal to or greater than s:

- The security strength provided by the asymmetric keys,

- The preimage strength of the hash function used in the HMAC construction, and

- The length of the derived key in bits.

5.4.2.2 Using HMAC in the Two-Step Key Derivation Process

SP 800-56C specifies a two-step key derivation procedure, which is also known as an "extraction-then-expansion" procedure. This procedure is included by reference in SPs 800-56A and B.

The extraction-then-expansion procedure in SP 800-56C is comprised of two separate steps: randomness-extraction and key-expansion, both of which can be implemented using an HMAC construction; when this construction is used, the same hash function is used for the randomness extraction and key expansion steps.

The security strength that can be provided by a key derived using the two-step procedure depends on the security strength of the asymmetric keys used to generate the shared secret, the preimage strength of the hash function used in each HMAC construction and the length of the derived key. In the randomness extraction step, the key used for HMAC is a salt, which can be a publicly known value, a secret value, or a combination of both; the result of this step is a key derivation key. In the key expansion step, the key used for HMAC is the entire key derivation key that was output from the randomness extraction step, e.g., if SHA-1 is used during the randomness extraction step, then the output is 160 bits in length, and is used as the key derivation key for the key expansion step.

When this two-step procedure is used, if a derived key is intended to provide s bits of security strength, then each of the following **shall** be equal to or greater than s:

- The security strength provided by the asymmetric keys,

- The preimage strength of the hash function used in the HMAC construction of each step of the procedure, and

- The length of the derived key in bits.

5.4.3 Using HMAC for Key Derivation from a Pre-shared Key

This section discusses and provides security requirements for the KDFs in SP 800-108 that are used to derive keying material from a pre-shared (i.e., existing) key, called a key-derivation key. HMAC can be used with an approved hash function to derive keying material.

The security strength of a derived key depends on the security strength provided by the key-derivation key, the hash function used in the HMAC construction and the length of the derived key. If a derived key is intended to provide s bits of security strength, then each of the following **shall** be equal to or greater than s:

- The security strength provided by the key-derivation key,
- The preimage strength of the hash function used in the HMAC construction, and
- The length of the derived key in bits.

5.5   Random Number (Bit) Generation

A random bit generator (RBG) is used to produce random bits. These bits may be used directly or may be converted to a random number (integer). Approved RBGs that use deterministic algorithms[5], along with methods for converting a bit string to an integer can be found in SP 800-90A. Other approved random number generators were either specified or approved by reference in FIPS 186-2 [FIPS 186-2]; however, their use is limited (see SP 800-131A [SP 800-131A]).

RBGs may be constructed using hash functions. The hash function used by the RBG **shall** be selected so that the RBG can provide a security strength that meets or exceeds the minimum security strength required for the random bits that it generates. See SP 800-57, Part 1, for the security strength that can be provided for each approved hash function for random number generation.

6   References

[SP 800-38B]	NIST Special Publication (SP) 800-38B, Recommendation for Block Cipher Modes of Operation: The CMAC Mode for Authentication, May 2005.
[SP 800-38C]	NIST Special Publication (SP) 800-38C, Recommendation for Block Cipher Modes of Operation: the CCM Mode for Authentication and Confidentiality, July 2007.
[SP 800-38D]	NIST Special Publication (SP) 800-38D, Recommendation for Block Cipher Modes of Operation: Galois/Counter Mode (GCM) and GMAC, November 2007.
[SP 800-56A]	NIST Special Publication (SP) 800-56A, Recommendation for Pair-Wise Key Establishment

---

[5] Commonly known as deterministic random bit generators or pseudorandom number generators.

	Schemes Using Discrete Logarithm Cryptography, March 2007.
[SP 800-56B]	NIST Special Publication (SP) 800-56B, Recommendation for Pair-Wise Key Establishment Using Integer Factorization Cryptography, August 2009.
[SP 800-56C]	NIST Special Publication (SP) 800-56C, Recommendation for Key Derivation through Extraction-then-Expansion, November 2011.
[SP 800-57]	NIST Special Publication (SP) 800-57, Part 1, Recommendation for Key Management: General, (Revision 3) July 2012.
[SP 800-90A]	NIST Special Publication (SP) 800-90A, Recommendation for Random Number Generation Using Deterministic Random Bit Generators, January 2012.
[SP 800-106]	NIST Special Publication (SP) 800-106, Randomized Hashing for Digital Signatures, February 2009.
[SP 800-108]	NIST Special Publication (SP) 800-108, Recommendation for Key Derivation Using Pseudorandom Functions, November 2008.
[SP 800-131A]	E. Barker and A. Roginsky, "Transitions: Recommendation for Transitioning the Use of Cryptographic Algorithms and Key Lengths", NIST Special Publication 800-131A, January 2011.
[SP 800-133]	NIST 800-133 Recommendation for Cryptographic Key Generation, (Draft), August 2011.
[SP 800-135]	NIST Special Publication (SP) 800-135, Recommendation for Existing Application-Specific Key Derivation Functions, Revision 1, December 2011.
[FIPS 180-4]	Federal Information Processing Standard 180-4, Secure Hash Standard (SHS), March 2012.
[FIPS 186-2]	Federal Information Processing Standard 186-2, Digital Signature Standard (DSS), January 2000.
[FIPS 186-3]	Federal Information Processing Standard 186-3, Digital Signature Standard (DSS), June 2009.
[FIPS 198-1]	Federal Information Processing Standard 198-1, The Keyed-Hash Message Authentication Code (HMAC), July 2008.
[SHA1 Attack]	Wang X., Yin Y., and Yu H., Finding Collisions in the Full SHA-1, The 25th Annual International Cryptology

Conference, Santa Barbara, California, USA, August 2005.

[Second Preimage Attack]   Kelsey J. and Schneier B., Second Preimages on n-bit hash functions for Much Less than 2^n Work, Lecture Notes in Computer Science, Vol. 3494, Springer, 2005, ISBN-10 3-540-25910-4.

[BCK1]   M. Bellare, R. Canetti, and H. Krawczyk, Keyed Hash Functions for Message Authentication, Proceedings of Crypto'96, LNCS 1109, pp. 1-15. (http://www.research.ibm.com/security/keyed-md5.html)

Appendix A : Actual Second Preimage Resistance Strengths of Approved Hash functions

In an application, if the size of the messages is small, then the second preimage resistance strengths of the hash functions are practically the same as their preimage resistance strengths described in Section 4.2.

The actual second preimage resistance strength for SHA-1, SHA-224, SHA-256 and SHA-512 is approximately $(L - M)$, where L is the output block size of the hash function, and the message is 2^M input blocks in length.

For example, if a message that is 2^{33} bits in length (i.e., a gigabyte long) is hashed by SHA-256 (whose input block size is 2^9 bits), the second preimage resistance strength is $(L - M) = (256 - 24) = 232$ bits (where $L = 256$, and $M = log_2(2^{33}/2^9) = (33 - 9) = 24$). That is, the amount of work required to find a second preimage is 2^{232}.

It is important to note that the amount of work is based on the number of compression function executions (compressing single message blocks), not on the number of hash function executions (hashing messages of more than one block in length).

The actual second preimage resistance strength of SHA-1, SHA-224, SHA-256 and SHA-512 varies, depending on the maximum size of the messages in the application using the hash function.

The second preimage resistance of SHA-384, SHA-512/224 or SHA-512/256 does not depend on the message length because the attack described in [Second Preimage Attack] would actually require more work than a brute-force approach, which will break the second preimage resistance of SHA-384, SHA-512/224 or SHA-512/256 with work of 384, 224, or 256 bits, respectively.

For any truncated message digest of λ bits, the actual second preimage resistance strength of SHA-1, SHA-224, SHA-256, and SHA-512 is the minimum of $(L - M)$ and λ, where $\lambda \leq 160$ for SHA-1, $\lambda \leq 224$ for SHA-224, $\lambda \leq 256$ for SHA-256, and $\lambda \leq 512$ for SHA-512.

The actual second preimage resistance strengths of SHA-384, SHA-512/224 and SHA-512/256 is λ (where $\lambda \leq 384$ for SHA-384, $\lambda \leq 224$ for SHA-512/224, and $\lambda \leq 256$ for SHA-512/256).

Appendix B : Document Changes

The original version of this document was published in February 2009. The main technical additions to this revision are:

1) Adding and addressing the security properties of SHA-512/224 and SHA-512/256.

2) Expanding the discussion of the security of HMAC values in Section 5.3,

3) Revising Section 5.2, especially sub-section 5.2.3 : Randomized Hashing for Digital Signatures, and

4) Section 5.4: Hash-based Key Derivation Function was rewritten to incorporate the "extraction-then-expansion" key derivation procedure specified in SP 800-56C and to discuss different approved hash-based key derivation functions.

www.ingramcontent.com/pod-product-compliance
Lightning Source LLC
Chambersburg PA
CBHW060515060326
40689CB00020B/4751